Inspirational One-Liners:
with Scripture
Aspire to Inspire & Motivate

Inspirational One-Liners II with Scripture: Aspire to Inspire & Motivate
Author & Published by Mignon Valliere Walker

Copyright © 2025 Mignon Valliere Walker
All rights reserved. No material of this book may be reproduced in any form without prior written permission from the copyright owner of this book.

The Scripture quotations taken from Holy Bible, New International Version ® NIV ®. Copyright © 1973, 1978, 1984, 2011 by Biblica, Inc.® Used with permission. All rights reserved worldwide.

For permissions contact: mignon.walker.1@gmail.com
Cover by Mignon Valliere Walker
ISBN: 978-0-9908789-9-5

**Giving ALL glory to God
I personally dedicate this book to:**

My husband: Adam. You are my God-sent in every way. Thank you for choosing to be the head of our household and accepting God's charge. You continue to luv me as Christ luv the church and stand with me to ensure our family serve the Lord.

My children: Janaevia, Jamohri, Jachin, and Javari. Remember you are born of GREATNESS, you are GREATNESS and are destined for GREATNESS!

I luv each of you unconditionally.

Inspirational One-Liners:
with Scripture
Aspire to Inspire & Motivate

My personal faith-based insights with added biblical scriptures have been written and shared with a purpose to uplift, inspire, evoke self-thought, self-reflection, energize and offer hope. Overall, this powerful, on-the-go, pocket-sized book is meant to inspire; encourage thought, motivation, and action. Share with friends, family, co-workers, colleagues, church family, and anyone needing encouragement.

II

1) The compassion of Christ is unmatched.

》 "When Jesus landed and saw a large crowd, he had compassion on them and healed their sick."
(Matthew 14:14)

II

2) God is not a GPS one gives orders; thy will be done.

**"This, then, is how you should pray: 'Our Father in heaven, hallowed be your name, your kingdom come, your will be done, on earth as it is in heaven.'"
(Matthew 6:9-10)**

II

3) Jesus will guide you; you must have faith, trust and believe.

❱ "Trust in the Lord with all your heart and lean not on your own understanding; in all your ways submit to him, and he will make your paths straight." (Proverbs 3:5-6)

II

4) God is not a limited resource. His abundance knows no bounds.

》 "And my God will meet all your needs according to the riches of his glory in Christ Jesus." (Philippians 4:19)

II

5) Don't let what you think you lack define you.

》 "But he said to me, 'My grace is sufficient for you, for my power is made perfect in weakness.'"
(2 Corinthians 12:9)

II

6) Place your cares into the hands of The One who is sovereign.

 "Cast all your anxiety on him because he cares for you."
(1 Peter 5:7)

II

7) Do not worry of those who abandoned you, if you have God, you are part of the majority.

》 "If God is for us, who can be against us?"
(Romans 8:31)

II

8) God is far greater than your situation; question is, do you truly trust Him?

⟫ "The Lord is my strength and my shield; my heart trusts in him, and he helps me." (Psalm 28:7)

II

9) I thank you Lord for what I already have.

》 **"Give thanks in all circumstances; for this is God's will for you in Christ Jesus." (1 Thessalonians 5:18)**

II

**10) Which one are you killing yourself to pay off, your....
a) debt to man/society
b) debt to Jesus (He already paid the price)**

》 **"You were bought at a price. Therefore honor God with your bodies."
(1 Corinthians 6:20)**

II

11) Let your mess be touched by the Messiah and turned into a message of hope which you may share with others.

》 "He lifted me out of the slimy pit, out of the mud and mire; he set my feet on a rock and gave me a firm place to stand."
(Psalm 40:2)

II

12) Jesus, Christ, Yahweh, Yeshuah, Messiah, the I Am Lord— He is all these and more.

》 **"Jesus Christ is the same yesterday and today and forever." (Hebrews 13:8)**

II

13) May it be done with courage.

》 "Be strong and courageous. Do not be afraid; do not be discouraged, for the Lord your God will be with you wherever you go."
(Joshua 1:9)

II

14) Jesus pushes you to the point you reveal your truth thus reveal His truth for He is the truth.

 "Then you will know the truth, and the truth will set you free." (John 8:32)

II

15) Struggling to find your identity; rest in the Lord and your identity shall be revealed.

》 "For you died, and your life is now hidden with Christ in God." (Colossians 3:3)

II

16) The best testimonies are of those of the broken and healed.

》 "He heals the brokenhearted and binds up their wounds." (Psalm 147:3)

II

17) If I must travel to your location for you to be a reliable and dependable friend, you're not a friend.

》 "The righteous choose their friends carefully, but the way of the wicked leads them astray." (Proverbs 12:26)

II

18) Satan out here trying to steal, kill and destroy families, stay in prayer.

**》 "The thief comes only to steal and kill and destroy; I have come that they may have life, and have it to the full."
(John 10:10)**

II

19) Choosing not to serve God will leave a bitter taste in your life; a bitterness that remains until you surrender to the Lord.

》 "Taste and see that the Lord is good; blessed is the one who takes refuge in him."
(Psalm 34:8)

(See Exodus: Moses & gold water)

II

20) Did God need to confer with Moses when He wanted to destroy the Israelites? No. God was angry, but this was a test of Moses's faith and his remembrance of God's promises to His people.

**》 "The Lord relented and did not bring on his people the disaster he had threatened."
(Exodus 32:14)**

II

21) God cares deeply about the sincerity of your heart.

**》 "People look at the outward appearance, but the Lord looks at the heart."
(1 Samuel 16:7)**

II

22) When God leads, there is nothing to fear.

》 "Even though I walk through the darkest valley, I will fear no evil, for you are with me." (Psalm 23:4)

II

23) Never question God's wisdom—those who do will face His correction.

**》 "The fear of the Lord is the beginning of wisdom, and knowledge of the Holy One is understanding."
(Proverbs 9:10)**

(See Numbers: Miriam questioning Moses)

II

24) Trust in the Lord, and He will guide you to meet your needs and fulfill the desires of your heart.

》 "Take delight in the Lord, and he will give you the desires of your heart." (Psalm 37:4)

II

25) Where is your faith and courage?

》 "Why are you so afraid? Do you still have no faith?"
(Mark 4:40)

II

26) How can you trust what another says about God's Word if you don't know His Word for yourself?

》 "Now the Berean Jews were of more noble character than those in Thessalonica, for they received the message with great eagerness and examined the Scriptures every day to see if what Paul said was true." (Acts 17:11)

II

27) Fear can keep you from God's Promised Land, just as fear kept the Israelites wandering for 40 years.

**》 "For God has not given us a spirit of fear, but of power and of love and of a sound mind."
(2 Timothy 1:7)**

II

28) Flesh frustrates flesh, but glory to God—there is peace in the Spirit.

》 "The mind governed by the flesh is death, but the mind governed by the Spirit is life and peace."
(Romans 8:6)

II

29) God does not appreciate a complaining spirit; instead, pray and be grateful for what you have.

》 **"Do everything without grumbling or arguing, so that you may become blameless and pure." (Philippians 2:14-15)**

II

30) My God, please forgive me.

**》 "If we confess our sins, he is faithful and just and will forgive us our sins and purify us from all unrighteousness."
(1 John 1:9)**

II

31) You cannot reach the Promised Land without effort on your part, for God gives the command and direction—you must listen and take action.

**》 "Do not merely listen to the word, and so deceive yourselves. Do what it says."
(James 1:22)**

II

32) The knowledge of God should be passed down from generation to generation.

**》 "One generation commends your works to another; they tell of your mighty acts."
(Psalm 145:4)**

II

33) God brought good out of my sadness.

》 **"And we know that in all things God works for the good of those who love him, who have been called according to his purpose." (Romans 8:28)**

II

34) Anyone who tries to attack me will stumble and fall.

》 **"Though an army besiege me, my heart will not fear; though war break out against me, even then I will be confident." (Psalm 27:3)**

II

35) Pray for the discernment to always do what is right.

》 **"Teach me good judgment and knowledge, for I believe in your commandments." (Psalm 119:66)**

II

36) Pure honesty inspires genuine healing.

》 "Therefore confess your sins to each other and pray for each other so that you may be healed." (James 5:16)

II

37) Do not profess something you do not possess.

》 **"They claim to know God, but by their actions they deny him." (Titus 1:16)**

II

38) Parents don't control your cans and cannots—you do.

》 "For we are each responsible for our own conduct."
(Galatians 6:5)

II

39) Life doesn't always mean joy, and death doesn't always mean pain.

》 **"There is a time for everything, and a season for every activity under the heavens: a time to be born and a time to die." (Ecclesiastes 3:1-2)**

II

40) Life leads to death, and death leads to life.

》 **"For to me, to live is Christ and to die is gain." (Philippians 1:21)**

II

41) To the enemy: Prepare to lose. Signed, The Conqueror.

》 "No, in all these things we are more than conquerors through him who loved us."
(Romans 8:37)

II

42) The shadow of the Almighty surrounds me—before, behind, and all around.

 "Whoever dwells in the shelter of the Most High will rest in the shadow of the Almighty." (Psalm 91:1)

II

43) The same yesterday, today, and forevermore: our Lord.

》 **"Jesus Christ is the same yesterday and today and forever." (Hebrews 13:8)**

II

44) There's blood on my hands if I don't tell you about our Savior.

》 "When I say to a wicked person, 'You will surely die,' and you do not warn them... I will hold you accountable for their blood." (Ezekiel 3:18)

II

45) Death shakes things up.

》 "For we know that if the earthly tent we live in is destroyed, we have a building from God, an eternal house in heaven."
(2 Corinthians 5:1)

II

46) Walk with the Lord and receive His abundant blessings.

》 **"Blessed is the one who does not walk in step with the wicked."
(Psalm 1:1)**

II

47) If you're not walking with the Lord but still think you're being blessed, those are residual blessings from someone connected to you who is walking with Him and praying fervently for you.

》 "The prayer of a righteous person is powerful and effective." (James 5:16)

II

48) Free will is not about two choices; there is only one choice: God.

》 "Choose for yourselves this day whom you will serve... But as for me and my household, we will serve the Lord." (Joshua 24:15)

II

49) Thy kingdom come, Thy will be done on earth as it is in heaven. To not choose God (life) is to choose death. Choosing death on earth means you will not exist in heaven.

》 "This day I call the heavens and the earth as witnesses... I have set before you life and death, blessings and curses. Now choose life."
(Deuteronomy 30:19)

II

50) When you observe sin in action, do not judge—PRAY.

 **"Do not judge, or you too will be judged."
(Matthew 7:1)**

II

51) Is it possible to live sinlessly? Repent and ask for forgiveness.

》 "If we claim to be without sin, we deceive ourselves... If we confess our sins, he is faithful and just and will forgive us."
(1 John 1:8-9)

II

52) JESUS.

》 "Salvation is found in no one else, for there is no other name under heaven given to mankind by which we must be saved."
(Acts 4:12)

II

53) There is only one way to life on earth and eternal life: no other choice exists.

⟩ **"Jesus answered, 'I am the way and the truth and the life. No one comes to the Father except through me.'"
(John 14:6)**

II

54) I AM (and you are) a vessel of creation.

》 "But we have this treasure in jars of clay to show that this all-surpassing power is from God and not from us."
(2 Corinthians 4:7)

II

55) Be self-controlled and alert; do not place yourself in a mind-altered state.

》 "Be alert and of sober mind. Your enemy the devil prowls around like a roaring lion looking for someone to devour." (1 Peter 5:8)

II

56) Wisdom only helps if you use it.

》 **"The beginning of wisdom is this: Get wisdom. Though it cost all you have, get understanding."
(Proverbs 4:7)**

II

57) Do what is good, right, and faithful before the Lord our God.

**》 "He has shown you, O mortal, what is good. And what does the Lord require of you? To act justly and to love mercy and to walk humbly with your God."
(Micah 6:8)**

II

58) Seek the Lord, work wholeheartedly, and you shall prosper.

**》 "But seek first his kingdom and his righteousness, and all these things will be given to you as well."
(Matthew 6:33)**

II

59) You are a child of the Most High God. Focus on the promise, not the problem.

》 **"The Spirit himself testifies with our spirit that we are God's children."
(Romans 8:16)**

II

60) Make God bigger than your problems.

》 **"Cast all your anxiety on him because he cares for you." (1 Peter 5:7)**

II

61) Persecution of the church will continue until the return of Jesus. Stand firm for Christ and in your faith.

》 **"In fact, everyone who wants to live a godly life in Christ Jesus will be persecuted." (2 Timothy 3:12)**

II

62) Say less than necessary.

**》 "Those who guard their
mouths and their tongues
keep themselves from calamity."
(Proverbs 21:23)**

II

63) Silence is the language of God.

》 **"The Lord is in his holy temple;
let all the earth be silent
before him."
(Habakkuk 2:20)**

II

64) Your healing is in the hem; your deliverance is in the hem.

**》 "She came up behind him and touched the edge of his cloak, and immediately her bleeding stopped."
(Luke 8:44)**

II

65) Structured by the Spirit.

》 **"Since we live by the Spirit, let us keep in step with the Spirit." (Galatians 5:25)**

II

66) Lack of faith makes one a wanderer, lost in the end, placing faith in many instead of the one true God.

 "But when you ask, you must believe and not doubt, because the one who doubts is like a wave of the sea, blown and tossed by the wind." (James 1:6)

II

67) The cycle of life: sin, judgment, repentance, faith, restoration.

》 "If my people, who are called by my name, will humble themselves and pray and seek my face and turn from their wicked ways, then I will hear from heaven, and I will forgive their sin and will heal their land."
(2 Chronicles 7:14)

II

68) Without God, everything is meaningless.

**"'Meaningless! Meaningless!' says the Teacher. 'Utterly meaningless! Everything is meaningless.'"
(Ecclesiastes 1:2)**

II

69) Honor God with both your heart and your lips.

》 **"These people honor me with their lips, but their hearts are far from me."
(Matthew 15:8)**

II

70) Place your trust and hope in the Lord, for He will never fail you as man will.

》 "It is better to take refuge in the Lord than to trust in humans." (Psalm 118:8)

II

71) Let your words and actions glorify Jesus.

》 "Let your light shine before others, that they may see your good deeds and glorify your Father in heaven." (Matthew 5:16)

II

72) Satan is always at work, assigning others to manipulate, intimidate, hoping you'll go against God's Word, sin, & give them a chance to discredit you. Be mindful, stay aware, & let God lead.

》 "Be strong in the Lord and in his mighty power. Put on the full armor of God, so that you can take your stand against the devil's schemes." (Ephesians 6:10-11)

II

73) "Don't go to flesh (man) for clarity; come to Me (the Lord), and I will use flesh as vessels to provide you answers," says the Lord.

》 "Call to me and I will answer you and tell you great and unsearchable things you do not know."
(Jeremiah 33:3)

II

74) To have a successful relationship with anyone—friend, spouse, or partner—you must have a relationship with God.

》 **"Unless the Lord builds the house, the builders labor in vain." (Psalm 127:1)**

II

75) If you have a relationship with God, your earthly relationships will succeed.

》 **"But the fruit of the Spirit is love, joy, peace, forbearance, kindness, goodness, faithfulness, gentleness, and self-control." (Galatians 5:22-23)**

II

76) "Jeshua is Lord." Believe in your heart and confess with your tongue.

》 "If you declare with your mouth, 'Jesus is Lord,' and believe in your heart that God raised him from the dead, you will be saved." (Romans 10:9)

II

77) If you walked through a forest in medieval knight armor, would you fear being harmed? In the same way, we should walk through this world wearing the armor of God.

》 **"Put on the full armor of God, so that you can take your stand against the devil's schemes." (Ephesians 6:11)**

II

78) You are the magic—believe in yourself.

》 "I can do all this through him who gives me strength." (Philippians 4:13)

II

79) Jesus, pray for me that my faith does not fail.

》 "But I have prayed for you, Simon, that your faith may not fail. And when you have turned back, strengthen your brothers."
(Luke 22:32)

II

80) Pray in the Holy Spirit, through Jesus Christ unto God the Father.

》 "But you, dear friends, by building yourselves up in your most holy faith and praying in the Holy Spirit, keep yourselves in God's love as you wait for the mercy of our Lord Jesus Christ to bring you to eternal life."
(Jude 1:20-21)

II

81) Light attracts light.

》 "You are the light of the world. A town built on a hill cannot be hidden... let your light shine before others, that they may see your good deeds and glorify your Father in heaven." (Matthew 5:14-16)

II

82) If you're breathing, you're in abundance.

**》 "The Spirit of God has made me; the breath of the Almighty gives me life."
(Job 33:4)**

II

83) With God, you can beat the odds.

》 **"With man this is impossible, but with God all things are possible."**
(Matthew 19:26)

》 **"I can do all this through him who gives me strength."**
(Philippians 4:13)

II

84) I am the righteousness of God in Jesus Christ.

》 **"God made him who had no sin to be sin for us, so that in him we might become the righteousness of God." (2 Corinthians 5:21)**

II

85) Christianity (teachings of Jesus) is God reaching out to man.

》 "But God demonstrates his own love for us in this: While we were still sinners, Christ died for us."
(Romans 5:8)

II

86) Comfort means help.

**》 "...the God of all comfort, who comforts us in all our troubles, so that we can comfort those in any trouble with the comfort we ourselves receive from God."
(2 Corinthians 1:3-4)**

II

87) Just know God, He loves you, He finds no fault in you, He delights when you come to Him.

》 "The Lord your God is with you, the Mighty Warrior who saves. He will take great delight in you... he will rejoice over you with singing." (Zephaniah 3:17)

II

88) Cherish yourself; love your uniqueness.

**》 "I praise you because I am fearfully and wonderfully made; your works are wonderful, I know that full well."
(Psalm 139:14)**

II

89) Renew your life; remove clutter.

**》 "Do not conform to the pattern of this world, but be transformed by the renewing of your mind..."
(Romans 12:2)**

II

90) Claim and declare your blessings; it's time to reap God's promises.

**》 "Let us not become weary in doing good, for at the proper time we will reap a harvest if we do not give up."
(Galatians 6:9)**

II

91) Quit feeding your fears and your doubt; feed your faith, you deserve to be free.

》 "For the Spirit God gave us does not make us timid, but gives us power, love and self-discipline."
(2 Timothy 1:7)

》 "So if the Son sets you free, you will be free indeed."
(John 8:36)

II

92) Hate (hyperbole) enough to prevent idolization and love unconditionally to share the Gospel.

》 "If anyone comes to me and does not hate his own father and mother and wife and children and brothers and sisters, yes, and even his own life, he cannot be my disciple." (Luke 14:26)

II

93) Grindin'...don't allow another to take you off your grind; it negates your hustle.

》 "Whatever you do, work at it with all your heart, as working for the Lord, not for human masters." (Colossians 3:23)

II

94) God.   Jesus.   Holy Spirit.
    Me.   Myself.   I.

》 "At that day you will know that I am in My Father, and you in Me, and I in you. He who has My commandments and keeps them, it is he who loves Me." (John 14:20-23)

- 1 Corinthians 3:16
  - Galatians 2:20
  - Romans 8:9-10

II

95) Those who are abandoned,
yearn to belong;
Those who are lonely,
yearn for a companion;
Those who are lost,
yearn to be saved;
Those who are lied to,
yearn for the truth;
Those who are flawed,
yearn to be flawless;
Those who feel unloved;
yearn to be loved;
Those who feel ugly,
yearn to be a swan;

(cont. next page)

(95 cont.)

II

Those who don't believe,
live with doubt;
Those who don't move,
live in fear;
Those who feel they can't win,
losing is always an option.

You do belong, You have a companion, You are saved, You have the truth, You are flawless, You are loved, You are a swan, You do believe, You do move, losing is NEVER an option for You already won! His name, Jesus!
(cont. next page)

II

95 cont.)
VICTORY comes by way of the unseen: faith, belief, hope!

》 **"Come near to God and he will come near to you. Wash your hands, you sinners, and purify your hearts, you double-minded."**
(James 4:8)

》 **"Come to me, all you who are weary and burdened, and I will give you rest."**
(Matthew 11:28)

II

96) The hardships within our trials and tribulation with continue until we fully incorporate Christ in our lives.

》 "My dear children, for whom I am again in the pains of childbirth until Christ is formed in you,..."
(Galatians 4:19)

II

97) We need not panic over the undergoing chaos and confusion in our lives. We need to rest in God. Prayer can prevent further chaos and confusion and promote healing. You/Me/We can take part in God's Glory.

》 "Yes, my soul, find rest in God; my hope comes from him."
(Psalm 62)

(cont. next page)

II

97 cont.)

》 "My soul finds rest in God alone; my salvation comes from him."
(Psalm 62:1)

》 "Yes, my soul, find rest in God; my hope comes from him."
(Psalm 62:5)

》 "My salvation and my honor depend on God; he is my mighty rock, my refuge."
(Psalm 62:7)

II

98) Your apology should match your changed behavior; if your behavior is unchanged then your apology was meaningless, pointless, empty, senseless, inane, insignificant.

》 **"Produce fruit in keeping with repentance."
(Matthew 3:8)**

II

99) Choose where you spend your time wisely; enforce boundaries for some are emotional and energy leeches.

**》 "Above all else, guard your heart, for everything you do flows from it."
(Proverbs 4:23)**

II

100) Sometimes we give the devil too much credit; majority of the time it IS you and your choices.

》 **"But each person is tempted when they are dragged away by their own evil desire and enticed." (James 1:14)**

II

101) Don't let your past (or past person) interrupt your new.

》 **"Forget the former things; do not dwell on the past. See, I am doing a new thing!"
(Isaiah 43:18-19)**

II

102) Those who believed lies about you can be bought with shillings for they will believe anything.

》 "The words of a gossip are like choice morsels; they go down to the inmost parts." (Proverbs 18:8)

II

103) You were not created to be pulled in two different directions.

》 "Such a person is double-minded and unstable in all they do." (James 1:8)

II

104) Go where you are appreciated and not tolerated.

》 **"If anyone will not welcome you or listen to your words, leave that home or town and shake the dust off your feet." (Matthew 10:14)**

II

105) Feeling Fabulous in (fill in the blank).

》 "There is a time for everything, and a season for every activity under the heavens."
(Ecclesiastes 3:1)

II

106) All that you strive for is coming together for your good.

**》 "And we know that in all things God works for the good of those who love him..."
(Romans 8:28)**

II

107) Focus on things that bring you joy and peace.

》 **"Whatever is true, whatever is noble, whatever is right... think about such things... And the God of peace will be with you."**
(Philippians 4:8-9)

II

108) Whom would you prefer to let down, God or family/friend?

》 "Anyone who loves their father or mother more than me is not worthy of me; anyone who loves their son or daughter more than me is not worthy of me."
(Matthew 10:37)

(cont. next page)

II

108 cont.)

》 "Am I now trying to win the approval of human beings, or of God? Or am I trying to please people? If I were still trying to please people, I would not be a servant of Christ."
(Galatians 1:10)

》 "Peter and the other apostles replied: 'We must obey God rather than human beings!'"
(Acts 5:29)

II

109) Do not give up, do not lose faith, remain righteous.

》 **"Let us not become weary in doing good, for at the proper time we will reap a harvest if we do not give up."
(Galatians 6:9)**

II

110) If what you do is pleasing to God, and serves goodness and luv, then that's all that matters.

**》 "Whatever you do, work at it with all your heart, as working for the Lord, not for human masters... It is the Lord Christ you are serving."
(Colossians 3:23-24)**

II

111) Try not to fall into temptation of creating your own tower of babel, ask God to show you what you need to see, to understand, what to do.

》 "Trust in the Lord with all your heart and lean not on your own understanding; in all your ways submit to him, and he will make your paths straight."
(Proverbs 3:5-6)

II

112) Once you are delivered from spiritual warfare, it is important to focus on spiritual hygiene.

》 **"Put on the full armor of God, so that you can take your stand against the devil's schemes." (Ephesians 6:11)**

II

113) God wants us to be as pure as we can be.

》 "Blessed are the pure in heart, for they will see God."
(Matthew 5:8)

》 "You are to be holy to me because I, the Lord, am holy, and I have set you apart from the nations to be my own."
(Leviticus 20:26)

II

114) Evaluate your actions and/or behavior.

》 **"Examine yourselves to see whether you are in the faith; test yourselves." (2 Corinthians 13:5)**

》 **"He repays everyone for what they have done; he brings on them what their conduct deserves." (Job 34:11)**

II

115) God, help me walk with you daily.

**》 "What does the Lord require of you? To act justly and to love mercy and to walk humbly with your God."
(Micah 6:8)**

II

116) Talk with God about everything (what should I do, now/next?).

》 "Do not be anxious about anything, but in every situation, by prayer and petition, with thanksgiving, present your requests to God." (Philippians 4:6)

II

117) God, bring the Scriptures of your Word alive in me.

》 "For the word of God is alive and active. Sharper than any double-edged sword, it penetrates even to dividing soul and spirit, joints and marrow; it judges the thoughts and attitudes of the heart." (Hebrews 4:12)

II

118) Your testimony has power.

**》 "They triumphed over him by the blood of the Lamb and by the word of their testimony..."
(Revelation 13:11)**

II

119) Let your actions reflect God's love.

》 **"Dear children, let us not love with words or speech but with actions and in truth."
(1 John 3:18)**

II

120) Stay rooted and grounded in God's Word.

》 "...continue to live your lives in him, rooted and built up in him, strengthened in the faith..."
(Colossians 2:6-7)

II

121) God will never stop loving you.

》 "...I have loved you with an everlasting love; I have drawn you with unfailing kindness." (Jeremiah 31:3)

II

122) God, teach me how to truly forgive and let go.

》 **"Get rid of all bitterness, rage and anger... Be kind and compassionate to one another, forgiving each other, just as in Christ God forgave you." (Ephesians 4:31-32)**

II

123) When you wholeheartedly accept/receive Jesus, there will be a fire inside you that you won't understand; you will be compelled to serve; you will witness change in self and those around you.

》 "But if I say, 'I will not mention his word or speak anymore in his name,' his word is in my heart like a fire, a fire shut up in my bones. I am weary of holding it in; indeed, I cannot."
(Jeremiah 20:9)

(cont. next page)

II

(123 cont.)

》 "Therefore, if anyone is in Christ, the new creation has come: The old has gone, the new is here!"
(2 Corinthians 5:17)

II

124) We are all experiencing different journeys; therefore, God speaks to each of us in different ways.

》 **"For God does speak—now one way, now another—though no one perceives it." (Job 33:14)**

II

125) It's okay to not understand all; there's a reason for everything & everything is in God's hands.

》 "'For my thoughts are not your thoughts, neither are your ways my ways,' declares the Lord." (Isaiah 55:8-9)

》 "And we know that in all things God works for the good of those who love him, who have been called according to his purpose." (Romans 8:28)

www.ingramcontent.com/pod-product-compliance
Lightning Source LLC
Chambersburg PA
CBHW050342010526
44119CB00049B/660